Bee Point Publishing
presents...

Tense.
Journey of an Unknown Poet
Where I've Been, Where I Am, Where I'm going

By: Bee Maree

Copyright

This is work from the heart. Pieces of me, but only pieces of me. To my past, my present, and my future self.
Any resemblance to actual persons, experiences or events is entirely coincidental.
Tense: Journey of Unknown Poet
is Published by Bee Point Publishing
First Edition

Copyright © 2017 by Poet Bee Maree
All rights reserved. No part of this book may be reproduced or transmitted in any form for any reason.

ISBN-13: 978-0692947425
ISBN-10: 0692947426

Table of Contents

Acknowledgment 8
Dedication 9
Two Places 10
Foreword 14
Where I've Been 17
A Lifetime Dream 18
A Never-ending Pain 19
A Wedding Vow 20
Cry No More 21
Dangerous 23
Diary 25
If Love Is Meant to Be 26
I'm a Girl 27
Just Like Me 29
Letting Go the Right Way 33
Life's Worth 34
Love Never Fails 36
Loving or Daring 39
Our Love Will Always Last 42
Relationships 43
Searching for Answers 44
Silent Nights, Lonely Days 45

Something So Special 46

Special One 47

Thoughts 48

Trapped 49

Why Should We? 50

Wish (Wishes) 51

Where I Am 52

Admiration 53

An Empty Drive 54

Ask Me Again 56

Backbone 60

Because of You 62

Devoted Time 65

Destined 66

Distraction 67

Empty 68

Fight Back 70

I'll Wait 74

Keep Making Memories 82

Love Recipe 83

Me! 84

Never Let You Down 85

Our Love 87

The Enemy 90

The "N" Crowd 92

The Only One 94
Love Can Be 96
Our Bond 97
What Happened? 99
Why I Love You 100
Unpredictable 101
Where I'm Going: 106
Blindsided- NPM #1 109
I'm trying to balance it 109
Fight's Not Over 114
Forbidden Crush 117
Expired 118
Here 119
Master's Journey 126
The Comeback 139
Weight 145
Why Me? 146
Why You 147

In memory of you Dee;
I know if no one would have supported me, you would have.
I love you and miss you more than these words can ever explain.
Fly high because God definitely gained an angel.

Delonna R. Williams 10/13/1982-09/21/2012

Tense: Journey of an Unknown Poet

"Feel where I've been, feel where I am, feel where I'm going
Just **FEEL** me..."

79 poems.
1 person's journey and endless emotions to tell it all.

My experiences have shaped me to tell this story
So tread lightly on this journey...
When you say that I am too much to handle just know I've been through a lot and it took so much just to get here.

--Bee Maree

Acknowledgment

A special thanks to you,
who helped me to pull a title out of the sky that would be known to script my world...
As I deal with your absence,
from it I have learned a great deal and I take with me lessons that will coast this unknown poet into the future; with higher standards, better values, self-respect and dignity that I foolishly gave up and you so selfishly robbed from me through a disguise called
LOVE.

Dedication

I dedicate my first collection of poetry
to anyone who has ever
inspired me and ignited my imagination
to write.
To those who have pushed me to pick
up a pen and etch my emotions into
paper,
To those who believed in my abilities
when I myself knew nothing of what
I possessed,
And lastly to those whose hearts my
poetry will touch and guide through
similar journeys.
Although I write for my own reasons, it
brings joy to my heart to know that
my poetry isn't just for me.

Love,
Bee Maree

Two Places

To my sister;
Hash that from another mister part because the lack of blood doesn't even begin to separate us from our love, so again I say to my sister.
The woman I strive to be like someday. My reflection of hard work, dedication, and hustle, cover to my book, as I am the inside of your pages and vice-versa.
I will forever cherish the friendship that we built so long ago,
from me being the brown nose fish to lesbian life and love...
and you,
you being the vibrant, sassy fierce bull that I would forever grow to love and aspire
to be like.
You believed, held my hand and watched me through many trials and journeys and even through your own battles still managed to cheer me on.

Even through the loss time we still managed to pick up in each other's lives as if we had never been absent and that is the moment that reassured true friendship for me. Through everything and the end of everything I will always be there and
you will always have two places with me;
My ART and my H.E.A.R.T.!

I love you Christiana,
Best Friend 4 Life!

In Just One Year

It took another 365 days of my life for me to find out who was for me and who wasn't.
Time, pain, and loss, yet still I was able to run into life's finest measurements of love.
God-fearing, vessels that never allowed me to give up on myself and that is the reason that I will forever love you both.
Friendship is overrated and not a soul can tell me that you aren't family, my family!
To stand by a stranger in a time of despair, and take me into your hearts when trying times made it hard to love yourself.
I just want you both to know that in just one year I have found every bit of strength, comfort, and unconditional love and there is no way for me ever to repay you other than to love you both in the way that you have loved me.

So, I dedicate my long-time work to you both because I know without your continued support I would not have finished this book. I love you guys!

Forever Love,

Bee

For you, Tiff H., a phenomenal woman and friend indeed and lastly, the woman who has stolen my heart Nissan G.

Foreword

By: Author Christiana Harrell

Tense: Journey of an Unknown Poet: Where I've been, Where I am, Where I'm going is the perfect title for this emotional collection of poetry. There is a little something for everyone to relate to between these pages. I have been a long-time friend of this poet and never have I seen her more vulnerable than on these pages. Bee Marie exposes parts of herself that most people only face when they are alone in darkness. One of the earlier pieces in the book mentions domestic violence between women, which can be a taboo thing. There is no fear or shyness in the words. I love how unafraid she is when it comes to telling her story through verse. I wish I could tell you a funny story about how we met, but the truth is, we'd gotten so close so soon, I'd never even noticed that she wasn't ever a part of my life. I hope that as people flip through these pages they see her as I do, even though this is only a glimpse of who she is and how impactful and infectious her energy is to everyone around her.

In all these years, she still has the biggest heart I've ever had the pleasure of crossing. We were both just young girls full of ambition and love when we crossed paths. Our stories in life are always on the same path—same characters, only with different names. We write each other's truths. For years, I have been encouraging Bee to publish these pieces for the world to read. She and I were both fairly young entering into the world of publishing and while I was a fiction writer, my first love was still poetry. She and I would sit and share for hours, critiquing the other as best we could—because there isn't much you can say when it comes to expression. I can remember her being that extra push that I needed in order to publish my very first novel that was a mixture of poetry and short stories. I was in a bad place and right out of a toxic relationship. Now, here I am ten titles and a nomination later ready to follow her through her publishing journey. I'm here to help her avoid the mistakes I made.

Be prepared to grow as you read. Bee's poems show clear cut emotions of how a girl becomes a woman through pain and love. A lot of poets and spoken word artist like to focus on political issues, but Bee has found her focus on the heart. I partly believe that the reason her work resonates with me is because love and pain have been my whole life. She wraps herself in people and allows herself to be inspired in situations that should lead to brokenness.

To my sister-friend, this is your time. Your moment to live and let love of self-uplift you. This book is the perfect place to start in doing you. Congratulations! Enjoy the ride.

A Verse from the Poet

Words are often hard to come by in a moment of expression,

so I write to relate to those of you who can find healings for your depressions,

through your smiles, your trials

As you push forward to validate your questions

For those who won't understand and for those who can bleed through the pen.

I write words to help bridge the pain that often cries for a hand

And to let you know I can relate just the same

Just as I write for you

It's also a cure to my pain.

Where I've Been:

(Hopscotch, Double-dutch, Tic-Tac-Toe)

A Lifetime Dream

A dream that still floats in the minds of us is
so vivid that it seems real
And everything that's fake seems so cute
you could feel
Feel the roughness of the concrete
or the edge of the grass
The smoothness of a person's face
The slickness of a glass
Yeah, things are great
You float on clouds
it's a dream
Everything's so wonderful, everything has
its means
It's great, it's fantastic,
too bad it's a fantasy
'Cause it hurts when I wake up knowing
you're no longer beside me.

A Never-ending Pain

I have this pain in my heart
And it won't go away
It hurts every morning and as I sleep the night away
It aches at every moment that I speak my mind aloud
If I tell someone I love them
Then that heart ache screams and shouts
It pounds and it pounds until it breaks me down in tears
And it's been doing that often like if there's something that it fears
It's very new to this feeling that keeps bullying my heart around
And every time it gets scared then it falls and hits the ground
This never-ending pain hurts
And it just won't go away
It's determined to be here forever
Until my heart's mate appears in fate.

A Wedding Vow

Here we are face to face
You heart is mine
Your soul to take
Your tears I cry,
My lips you kiss
The vows are placed below this list:
"Together… we are
What others could have never experienced
Me and you…
Something others…
Would have loved to deny,
but we live to tell what has become of our lives,
To lead to this special day…
You take away—me
And I…I take in me—you!
You! You! As my King!
My Everything!
~I Love You~"

Cry No More

As the day passed by
And the clouds drifted on
Memories came to my head
Remembering my grandmother wasn't home
Tears sprung to my eyes
As my heart crashed in pain
I couldn't hold it in anymore
I still couldn't understand
I know when it's time to go
You have to do what you have to do
But, no one ever asked me
If I ever needed you
Well I do
But I know that you can't come back
But couldn't HE have waited two or three years
Or even more, so we could chat?
I miss you grandmother
And I really need you by my side
Til' it clearly comes to me that I will no longer have to cry
And when that day comes and someone can be so sure
Then I'll realize that I have to cry no more

Tense: Journey of an Unknown Poet

Dedicated to anyone who has ever lost a Grandmother

Dangerous

When I first met you, I thought
you were the one
Then you left me for this chick
now our relationship is done
You crushed me deeply, now I
weep and cry
Looking so sad, wishing I die
But, now I'm over you, tears
and all
There's more than you, there's
more than ball
So now I know why not to fall
in love
It's because of people like you
that cause all of this, all of the
above.
So I leave this in the past,
present, and future
Not the least worried about you
Cause you're dangerous in
many ways
I've wasted too many days
On someone like you
Who wasn't even cute

Like the ol' saying goes
"there's plenty of fish in the sea"
So let me go, let me be.

Diary

Diary,
I missed you today
And the little time we got to talk, it wasn't much, but it brightens up my face
I like that you listen and you take the time to understand
I see that in my life you could be the "better man"
If "HT" were taken off of "heart" and ear was all that was left
Would you listen to the beat of the love and this relationship itself?
If you care, do you dare, to test your love with a match, that's the catch…
    Hear me if you love,
    Equip me if you love,
    Arrange us if you love,
   Rescue me if you love and
Together we can do it cause it's nothing but
      LOVE.

If Love Is Meant to Be

If love is meant to be,
Will the L, let me know,
If love is meant to be,
Will the O, open doors,
If love is meant to be,
Will the V, vow before me,
If love is meant to be,
Will the E, ever let me breath,
If love is meant to be,
Will you show me how it is?
Because LOVE should be treated fairly,
Cause it's nothing but a gift.

I'm a Girl

I'm a girl with potential
I'm a girl with class
I'm a girl with style
And I'm one to make things last
I'm a girl with dreams
And I'm willing to make them come true
I'm a girl with skills and I'm nothing like you
I'm a girl that's smart that's looking for things in life
I forget about all the wrong things and then I do what's right
They have all the girls in this world that try to be like me
But, I stand here and tell them that they could never be
Then my life drifts to that spot where I want it to float
Where my life points to my future and I can no longer coast
I'm a girl that's beautiful on the inside and out
I'm a girl that expresses herself even if I have to shout
I'm a girl that's proud for the things I do

And I'm nice and thoughtful and independent too
I don't depend on people to do for me
I work with people and encourage them
And when they need help they call on B.
I'm not a violent girl, I don't like to fight
I only fight when I need to and that's when things are right
I'm a girl with a weakness just like anyone else
But, my weakness is way different, and I'm not myself
My weakness at this point is so…
It's so sweet
I can't tell you at this point but I can let you know that this weakness sets me free
Well I can no longer state what type of girl I am to be
But if this poem was to continue and you were to read it you would see
I'm just me.

Just Like Me

I am a self-centered person
I'm in control of myself
I have the power to succeed like nobody else
I am strong, I am beautiful
I have the ability to strive
I avoid all the wrong and do what's right
I'm the seed from the ground,
I'm the sun in the sky
I'm the mighty hawk that soars through the clouds in the night
I'm precious, I'm sweet
I can manipulate the mind
I can guide the brain to conduct experiments the size of a dime
I'm like the earth on a daily basis
I make my turns year round
And I'm always standing strong
You'll never see me fall down
I'm the world as you see it
So take a good look and see
That this personality is in you as it is
Just like me.

Just Listen

My history flows pass me like the river in the valley
I see many young leads trying to score the big fee
But I never let the black war carry on too far
I'll never forget what our black heroes achieved
I'll always remember what our generation today needs to succeed
After ROSA, MALCOLM X and the KING himself
You'd think that the drama could never take place again…
But, their words only rang in the ears of the true people who cared to listen
We still get treated differently because of our skin color
Especially our males assuming that drug dealers only live past our black brothers
When they scoring from the white man
The blue-eyed, skin tan
Never expecting he poppin' that "X"
Only black people are suspects in the eyes of the "necks"

And shoplifters only exist on struggling *sistahs'*
Only trying to survive on the food stamps and wishes
Yet, they dismiss us,
Cause of skin color, our hair texture, our tone
What's wrong??
Are we not good enough because we're black to the bone??
Are you *drove* because some of us still have the will-power to coast?
And make it a toast because we still believe in the matters we host
Our elders screwed up because they show us the road that we imitate, and replicate, and make our own
And the little of us that keep hopes high in heart, departs, to keep our mentality strong
Are you listening, our generations to come are here to make things glisten
Raising the bar, and climbing; making new legacies
Looking forward to new plans and obstacles
So stop what you're doing
And just listen

Katrina Survivors

Kissed it goodbye
At least
Thinking we'd be
Right back. Never knew
I'd never see
New Orleans
As home again.
Struggling, trying to close my eyes and imagine it
Uttering constantly, it's a dream, a horrible nightmare
Realizing my all is gone
Visioning my days in my backyard, now
Involuntarily a polluted river
Viciously tearing my city, my HOME, a part.
Oh how not even my tears can describe the pain
Ripping me inside… Thankfully though I'm a Katrina
Survivor.

Written as an English Assignment in, 2005, for the victims of Hurricane Katrina.

Letting Go the Right Way

The future will be too late
and the past is already gone
So today is the right time to tell you
what a special friend you are
You were always there to say something
rather than just a simple nod or smile
And that took away the doubt I felt at least
for a little while
Telling you I'll only miss you
would only make me want to cry
And saying goodbye would make it forever
So I'll say see you next time
I won't tell you I'll keep in touch with you
'cause that only means I really won't
So I'll say see you tomorrow cause it's the
right way to let you go!

Dedicated to: Kristi

Life's Worth

What's worth living if we can only dream
the good things and live the worse?
Taking every step carefully, seeping deep
down as it hurts
Is it worth a day in life to never know when
dangers around?
Or have the sense of looking into the killer's
eye before you hit the ground
Wanting love, a better life, or just to flee
away from here
Trying to make a way through mazes,
standing strong with nothing left to fear
Wondering will you ever make the next day
to enjoy it like your last
Having flashbacks of the times, sweet
memories of your past,
What is the meaning of life, if we only live
here just to die?
And the death breaks down the hearts of the
ones we love, then they cry
For us to be back on this earth, which we so
gradually flew away
And on their knees, they fall on the ground,
screaming and praying in sorrowful pain

So tell me "life's worth" if it only issues hard times,
When we could live up in the ghetto and serve the time for the crime
Is life's worth just a visual moment to experience what you see
'Cause if it's that then I'm pleased
Because "life's worth" is what's me.

Love Never Fails

Love never fails to hurt you
Is there a purpose for this virtue?
Spending days and nights searchin'
For the chance in this person
So blinded by the light that your own words hurt you
Waking up stressing, feeling that this
Blessing is testing your patience
How much more can you take without fakin'
Mind so blown, it's hard to pull back
Heart constantly aching, this pathway is fading
Love is falling off track
Fed up with the love that never shows back
Driftin' makes you want it more,
Wanting more makes you wants to drift
So tired of this switch,
the testing never seems to quit,
Honestly feeling like you've reached the end
No comparison, no other could ever fit the script
Eyelids filled with pain, hard to push aside
Emotions rising high, heart vibes higher than the sky

Not enough hours in the day to show how much you care
So many tears, worthless fears, no longer feeling you're there
Playing the role of a clown, only to keep the sorrows down
Patiently waiting, barely escaping, must be crazy
Telling yourself so much that it's worth it
Something so fresh, no longer so perfect
Giving love a try, issuing your heart with many purpose
Only ending up suffocating, hearing yourself repeat that you're tired of this hurting
Telling yourself you can do it
But the actions barely prove it
Too hesitant to take a step, clueless of what's holding you back
Not here to waste your time, just looking for some kind of sign
Assuring that your love is here voluntarily
Knowing you're here to stay keeps the sun shining fairly
Visions of sweet kisses, dreamingly I worship
Understanding that if it's true

Love never fails to work it.

Dedicated to: J. Fields

Loving or Daring

To love, to hate,
to form, to break
to live, to die,
to strive, to cry,
What is expected?
What does it take?
To prove what is true,
And who are the fakes
How am I treated?
Why am I dissed?
From the world itself, but my love insist
That I'm thrown to the ground and shattered like trash
Piled up like dust, and blown away like ash,
Why? Why?
Is the question I seek,
No answers from Him more questions from me
Am I done at this point?
Is there something left here?
More disappointments?
Lose faith, bring more sorrowful tears
Where I leak …
And I leak
And I leak all the way through

Look what has happened, what can I do?
Kill...
Kill who? Kill me? No, Kill you!
Daring, attempting, loving all of that
The temptation is calling, but angels call back
Do I cry? Do I lie? Stop trying? Say goodbye?
Where do I turn in this self-taking strive?
How can I paddle my way through the forbidden seas?
How do I receive my treasure that was set for me?
To retrieve from the devils when my heart was destroyed
No man can stand here and say they're here for no wrong
Not all men are alike but have similar greed's
To break you a part is their ultimate dream
For them to be king, and you under their feet
Treat you as a servant and never as their Queen
Loving or Daring, it's a struggle for the both
When turns bring you to the center it's difficult to vote

Love should be the seed that grows through every human being
While dare, be the, adventure,
that takes them to view the things they've never seen
Now the choice shouldn't be difficult
You should have an idea of yourself
And treat the open public with nothing but respect.

Our Love Will Always Last

The day could fall apart.
And the world could crumble to ash
But as long as we have each other
Our love will always last.

Relationships

Relationships are like fire they burn when they are destroyed
Then that young girl and that young boy disappears from the world
Relationships are like ice they melt when they are hot
When a couple gets turned on they hit each other's spot
Relationships are like a cool pool, when you take a dip it's smooth
When couples argue they are not in the mood,
But to sit down and talk to smooth things out is what a special relationship is all about.

Searching for Answers

Even though you know that my love is broken down
My heart is torn, my blood is weak
Because you aren't around
And even when I say I hate the ground you chose to walk
I blame myself for losing you, it's hardly all your fault
As everyday arises I try to simply see
The reasons why you hurt the heart that only cared to beep
Although, I can't realize what signs have been set for me
I'll continually search for answers that only I can see.

Silent Nights, Lonely Days

The silent nights I spend alone
The lonely days that don't belong
The days I wish that you were here
The things I'd whisper in your ear
You are special to me in every way
Wish you were here on this glorious day
To give away the special things we share
Is something I dare
I dare not do to you or me
To keep the things that are sacred in my heart
And make sure they never get out , never depart
So if you're gone, it's okay
We'll meet again, we'll meet someday!

Something So Special

Something so special that you should cherish and keep
Something you breathe every night as you sleep
Something that shines like a jewel in the sun
Something so precious, something that's done
A life full of excitement is the best of all times
Something that's yours that could also be mine
Something that could hurt if you walked out of my life
Or crush you in the darkness of the medieval fights
Something that kills that has been blessed by a God
Something that's reality and also that's odd
Something so special and something so right
What you couldn't live without is the soul of your life.

Special One

Boy you are that special one I dare not speak your name
I'll take you in and you'll be mine but please don't play that game
I'll trust you with my heart and soul and give you all you need
You do me wrong, I'll get you back and you'll be on your knees.
Boy you are that special one you are all I need
No one can do the things you do and all those special deeds
And if you ever break my heart or lie to me again
You'll swear you never met me 'cause your life will come to an end
Boy you are that special one I dare not do you wrong
Cause someone special just like you should and always will be strong
So never worry about things I tell you in this special poem
Cause I'll treat you how you want to be treated and then I will be gone.

Thoughts

As I sit in this bed
Thoughts run through my head
Words, phrases, mommies, babies
As the day goes by there's not much to do
I'd rather spend the rest of my life with you
Do you feel the same? Can you feel my pain?
I really wish people would stop playing games
Blacks, whites, cards, dice
All of these things glisten like ice
Thoughts of the world, thoughts of all kinds
I really wish that you were mine
Be my boyfriend, I'll be your girl
I'll be your everything
 I'll be your world.

Trapped

Growing in a world filled with sex, drugs, and hate
It's nothing you can do to change the way it operates
You're trapped,
You have no way out
All you can do is live the tale
We livin' life temporarily in the underground world
Workin' for the devil's team
Until our savior takes His people
And rewards them with the pleasure of staying in a land
Where you are bound to be free
Until then you're trapped in a hatred shed
Where we cry, scream, spit, and bled
We are to suffer until our sins are forgiven
And the one from above, lets us enter heaven.

Why Should We?

Why should we wake up every day to see the sunrise?
When it goes away at night and the moon is all that shines?
Why should we create minds to use, when only our intelligence gets ignored?
And we're turned away to leave on the way out you hit the door
Why should we cherish every day and try to teach this life and survive?
Why should we actually try to search the secret finer things in life?
Why should we travel up the last step just to keep our world in line?
When we only wait for judgment day to tell the world goodbye?

Wish (Wishes)

Boy I wish that you were here
To wipe up all these sorrowful tears
To take me in your arms one day
And tell me everything will be okay
How I wish to tell you so
The things that go on without you though
The things that happen all so quick
The things that take just one lick
To continue on day and day
To try to make it through, make my way
To follow the paths through the garden
And all of these mazes make me harden
To see your face would make me smile
To make it there would take awhile
But as long as you stay by my side
There's nothing that can override
My thoughts and feelings hurt too much
And all I wanna do is touch
Touch your face, see your eyes
Just thinking about it makes me wanna cry
Well now you know just how I feel
So get it together, you know the deal.

Tense: Journey of an Unknown Poet

Where I Am: (desire, affliction, growth)

Admiration

I know strong ...
but I've never seen anyone in action as
strong as you.
Although the days have been trying
giving up is something you haven't done
I'm so proud of the woman you have
become
your mom IS proud too
and as she looks down she knows she did
fine by you
as you continue to walk in the path that God
guides you to
Adding on to a legacy that HE will see you
through.

An Empty Drive

Lately I see you running...
Now-a-days when I turn my back
and I'm looking to be covered
I see the dust
rising...
Kicked up from your feet down under
As you beat the pavement with the limbs
that God gave you to run with...
-light chuckles-... I knew I should've seen
this shit coming
When your behavior started to steer
And I could sense that your fear was
becoming
Just never knew it would be me that you
decided to scroll, select, and delete from
I understand the capacity may be
overflowing
But the purpose of your secure digital (SD)
card is to move your most important articles
into a place of safety
Not dispose of them...
Perhaps you are mistaking your bejeweled
jewels for spam
Confusing the unwanted thirty days trial
with your lifetime warranties span

Allowing the battery to deplete to empty
Conditioning your energy to barely hold
charge at the start of every day's beginning.
misjudging the normal wear and tear
for damages beyond repair--
Replacing your lifeline with the newest
piece of equipment out there...
Just covering up the blemishes
Concealing your insecurities
Dressed in labels to impress your enemies...
Making appearances to entertain these bitches...
Hmm... don't forget who knows the outside of you and all of your interior...
It just kills me how you are so attention driven.

Ask Me Again
This open discussion led to a question
One so unclear to me until I took the time to listen
So… ask me again, would you?
So that I can properly address it
with no hesitation….
See lately, I've been so wrapped in your sensation
And even though my lips rarely say it
I appreciate the love that you show me on a daily.
You seem to put me in a place I've never been
The joys of sharing kisses with my best friend
Security that holds me down to the very end
Yeah…
This is that "real love" feeling
-sighs- .. silly in love
So addicted to your bear hugs
I've never felt so open
You're the prize and I'm the token
Collecting my winnings…
Like a $5 Monday night blackjack…
Constantly doubling on them tens

But seriously if the sky opened up and rained endlessly
I would dance with you to the rhythm of the lightning and thunder
Because I'm just that into it…
This you
This me
This is
Loyalty and trust
Two of the hardest things to come by
And in a matter of ALMOST 152 DAYS
We've managed to handle each other's dark skies
Riding on the steel rims bent side
But still riding
Amazing how another can bring out the best in me
You don't just shade in my inner circle
You paint the world with me
Exposing my flaws outside of the lines
Using every color to criticize
In the attempt to see us both rise
We grind
Even in the worst of moods I still awake
Excited because of your smile
The reason I spit

Is because you give it meaning to fit
And I continue to strive
I've never had a woman to compliment my lifestyle
With our differences
A space to be messy
And the sense of humor to match my silliness
That one look in my eyes that can describe my happiness
Even when I feel the crappiest
It's never a dull time
With you…
Blue is never blue
And I can never stay mad at you
For long---
"No Matter What" … I'm just hearing our song
Replay
Ironic that you would introduce it
And that I would become so use to it
And five months later we live it fluently
And I'm right back to loving you
No matter the aim
You're the joy to my rain
And when I'm in pain--my cure

This love is so pure
There is no doubt.. for me at least
Not an ounce in me "unsure"
In fact I'm more than positive
Even if God hasn't placed you here to ride it out with me
Not a single day would be lived with regret
It was all done in happiness
You genuinely make me HAPPY
No fronts for the net
Just real L.O.V.E
You put it out there for the world to see
So when you ask me again
This is the value you bring to me.

Backbone

I hold your hand in spirit
Because no amount of words spoken
Or actions tokened
Can heal the space that feels so broken
I know the feeling...
Easy to build the memories
So hard to think of them dwindling....
Everything that once seemed so sound
Now bellows in the empty pit of your skull
No words to speak,
no appetite to eat
Unspoken questions
Leaves your heart searching for answers
Deadbeats ...
I wish there were a way to erase the pain you feel inside
For it hurts me to see you hurt through your eyes
This emotional breakdown seems to steal your smiles through your silent cries
And joy seems so far away rather than near by
But in due time...
All of the pieces will connect for its purpose
And when you're hurting

The world will be to blame
The unexplained will drive you insane
The grieving process will be the hardest adjustment to tame
But no matter what I'll be here to stand
Holding you-- hand in hand
Helping you cope
When nothing matters the most
I'll hold you close
I'll cup your tears and reassure you there is nothing to fear.
And if you know nothing else
When nothing seems clear
When the trial seems like it's far from getting better
Just know we will battle it together!

.

Because of You

It's because of you
I smile…
That even on the bluest of days
You still manage to help me let the sun shine through
You hold me down when I'm low
And raise me higher when I'm flying over the open sky
You are the motivation to my reasons why
You don't build me
You build with me
You see things I never thought could become of me
The reason I stick to this "us" theme
This "us" team
A vision of forever
You and me looking past the stormiest weather
You bring out the best
The rhyme
The sparkle in my eye
And I sit back to reflect on just how time
Has allowed us to bond
My lips don't ever have to speak
My heart recites rhythms from its beats

Emphasizing a love so deep
That I had to write it on this sheet
Loving the fact that I'm for you and you're for me
5-15-13

Defeated

I'm starting to think that this is magic
You make my heart melt; can't you tell it?
What you hold in your hands,
that lies to rest in my chest seems to beat to
the rhythm of a love spell
My heart seems to be on a repeat for a refill
Wanting all of you, every single detail
And lawd, your tongue seems to work real well
Letting the words run so smoothly when you spill it
Better yet speak
The back of my knees stay weak as I
continue to fall for your love, deep
I tell you
love always seems to defeat me.
I love you.
4-25-13

Devoted Time

Something to look back on
Infamous pose
Lyrics that move you
Music so bold
Hearts that unravel
Blood so thick
Fantasies forever
Love so perfect
Flaws imperfect
Imperfect; perfect enough
Dreams so vivid, can't get enough
Not enough said
Too much said is a mess
We all dream of love
Which doesn't EXIST!

Destined

I can't explain it
And if I had to
I would do it all over again
Just to be right here standing...
Next to her
Some may think of it as moving too fast
But there's no limit to love or measurement of it lasting
Instantaneous emotions have been constantly flashing since day one
we've been in sync
Destined to make it last!

Distraction

Why don't I ever follow my first mind?
When the vibe told me you weren't shit?
Yet I let you spit
And wet up my pussy because the bill fit—
You were a ho' and changing wasn't even an option...
I know
I played in the open field
Blind to what I thought was real
I just knew this was nothing more than a distraction
3-15-13

Empty

The pit…
The pit of my stomach can't even spit out my image
My eyes can't even fill up to cry out these feelings
Driftin…
Pass these minor setbacks,
Wishin' they pass
Softly reminiscing…
But snap back quickly to reality of how blessed I've been
And even though the growth of the pain is intense
I've learned to look past the end which opens doors to my beginning
My lips quiver
they can barely sync the words
Making conversation that is
My knees buckle at every thought of this
This emptiness...
My tears are invisible
So, they ride the lining of the bottom lashes
Burning my skin as they crash
Emotions and secrets buried so deep inside
Wanting to vent but the pride overrides

Wanting so bad to scream out, crack up, blow down
But holding in all the inner me
Smile on the face, heart with a frown
My screams go unheard, so I'm mute as if nothing is wrong
Shadowed in the dark hoping no one sees me cry alone

Fight Back

She says all we do is
Fight…fight… fight...
And you're right
We've put in too much blood, sweat, and tears
Literally...
Not to battle for our lives
Together...
Taking care of each other for the better
The thought of fighting with someone
Never seemed so clever
I'd do it all over again just to be in this position
No single day is promised so let's cherish every step to the building of this mission
and no, we can't fight off this tumor
And no matter the rumor
I refuse to let your faith die down with the foolishness
No one can make those decisions but our ruler
It's neither our place to question or suggest a better time or even how
So yea...
Lets fight for her to see better days

It counts
every second, minute and hour that he's
blessing us with right now
I admire your courage and strength
At such a young age
In this trying stage
It takes a warrior to transition and step up to
the plate
You have nothing but my loyalty and the
utmost respect.
There's no other base I'd rather play
Than your catcher on the back cage
Catching your heart, breaking your fall
Holding you close when the world seems so
cold
Reassuring you
As the story unfolds
Shading your darkest areas with a hint of
bel-air soles
Striving for smiles that we most often hold
Back... into a corner as life turns us over
But it isn't over
Our path paves a way for us to keep on
strolling
Even with the season taking a toll on us
physically and mentally

Letting the devil have his way and steal our joy spiritually…
Isn't an option
You will still push forward with her legacy
Walk forward with your head up and gracefully
I'll make sure of it baby
Just know as long as you're still breathing
She's synched to you and it keeps her presence alive and her heart still beating
So there's no reason to feel defeated
I have your back
There's no question in that

Heart Therapy

Writing the words that I can't speak have become the medicine to my pain
Again, and again
I overdose on the sayings
Writing my words, my thoughts, my feelings
Getting deeper than the blue sea on winter frost evening
I'm growing daily
And with each step
I'm able to make a way
Carving out the lessons learned from each heartbreak

I'll Wait

They say distance makes the heart grow fonder-- I hope it's true :(
I go crazy at night thinking of you-- thinking of us-- fading
I found a letter at the bottom of my purse that you gave me...
7 weeks after so much pain you still found a way to enslave me...
into your heart
I take pride in *jocking* your slang
And quoting you from the start:
"I took you for granted,
I stepped on your heart...
And the only thing that can put it back together is time....
No "I love you", no "I'm sorry", no "I promise" just time.... "
So fine....
I hear time heals everything
So in time...
I'll wait
Another line from you said that I stepped out on faith... but you did to bae...
"I love you...
a love that's so scary,

because it happened oh so fast,
A love that's so emotional because we both fear hurt
But you stepped out on faith bae
You gave me your worth
You took care of me day after day
......night after night"
"..... so don't give up on love and if your heart tells you different, then don't give up us…"
Even when we wanna walk
Shutdown and don't wanna talk
You gotta fight
And I will never let you fight alone
Yes, it's been a rocky road
And neither of us knows what tomorrow holds...."
I was serious when I told you, your words meant everything...
I hold them close to my heart just to fight off the enemy...
The REAL reason that I fight
Is because you promised me the battle wouldn't be a one man-hype...
.... so we sacrifice...
No complaints, no restraints

Just patience into the next case...
Willing to battle the setting of the night and the rise of the day
And in time our paths will intertwine
We will get back to grinding and pushing over time
Coping with decisions...
As if nothing seems different...
So until then... I'll wait!

Just Another Fight

You know it's nights like this
Where I lay awake
With tears streaming down my face
That I craved to hear your voice on the other end
Tell me it would be ok
Or that you were ready to ride
To put a bitch in her place
You loved me that much
Your touch
Made the difference
Your hand on my shoulder
Your hug was always warmer
And no matter what you always had my back
Can I be honest?
I've missed you
For that
I have faced lonelier days
But the absence of your presence felt like eternity flames
I tried to replace you
Let me back up...
Did you get it?
I...

tried to replace
YOU…
Now let's be real here for a second
I couldn't
There was no other that could walk in the same pair of heels in the way that you strutted
I was so angry and displaced
But the hurt
Is really what consumed my face
My eyes
My tongue
My gut
My heart
When it ended I was past the angry part
I wanted to plunge at the time
Because every time I opened my eyes
I saw you...
I kept thinking it was a sign
To force my stubborn behind
To reach out
But shouted back to feeling betrayed
And how there was no way
I would do it
Who knew
Time would fly by

And my stubborn behind
Would miss out on so much
The days I would lay awake
Dealing with some childish charade
And needing the wisdom of my best friend
To push me past my stubborn ends
Words cannot begin to express
How lost I have been
I never truly understood the phrase of
"losing your best friend "
Never thought of our bond as loose ends
Maybe tense
But shit we had dabbled down that road before
just not the path less traveled
Nothing like this
I tried with her
But she failed me
I tried confiding,
And crying,
But nothing comforted my inner lining
But this was
Just another fight, right?
At least we thought it was
Soon to be reconciled with bear hugs

And right back to picking up where we left off
-shrugs-
Or not...
Stubborn Bull and Capricorn hooves
Seem to play tug a war
Until somebody folds
But not once did I stop thinking of you
Many nights of blue
made me wish
I could lay in your bed
And cry my eyes out
To hear you say it would be ok
But time faded away
And the realization made it clear
It wasn't just another temporary day
A little over a calendar year
Still lingering with fear
Battling with a decision
Of whether to reach out
Make a call,
Send a message
Or nothing at all
Just struggling to get past the door
Not sure if my key fit anymore
The turn and click of the knob

Made my heartbeat throb
And pushing my way through the door
Released the pressure I could no longer endure
Greeted by that same familiar cure
For a heartache
Expressions of forgiveness
And picking up as if it was just yesterday's business
I've missed that
Those joyful days filled with laughter that carried through the night
Is it safe to say?
Once again this was
just another fight ?

Keep Making Memories
People always start off peachy!
Cooking, cleaning,
romancing, and such and then eventually
they get tired…
or comfortable
they stop doing all that they did to get you ,
to keep you.
I wonder why?
It would appear to me that the relation
would grow boring
so why wouldn't people attempt to try
something "new" at every opportunity.
Try to keep the love alive
I don't ever want to get tired ,
I just want to keep making memories
to write "our" story
4-17-13

Love Recipe

Love letters,
small tokens of appreciation
Just because notions,
love potions,
Joy, excitement
Butterflies in the tummy, passionate kisses
Sweet misses, (I miss you)
Long stroking
Mesmerized, long goodbyes, tight hugs
Back rubs, play fights
Karaoke, dance with the wind
Perform from within
Role play, encourage, inspire, desire,
motivate, bond, never stop building memories
4-17-13

Me!
Who am I?
What are these?
Who are you?
Where are we?
Who is this?
What is love? Without a couple there to seek?
Am I depressed? Am I lonely?
Do I need some help?
What is this world that's ending?
What is this home we live in?
What did I do? Is it wrong?
The help is needed to make me strong
Am I me? Or someone else?
Can I change or be depressed?
Can you help find
Me?

Never Let You Down

This isn't a come back
Or that when your eyes lay upon it
you think I'm fighting fire with fire
Even with all of our desires,
I'm not spiteful
I just often wonder,
Am I still the figure placed in this season to help you get over her?
She is gorgeous and I know she still holds your heart
I wonder if that's what keeps us apart
Or is it my baggage?
The one you were so eager to handle
I just can't help but wonder are we serving as replacements
On a day to day basis
Beating pavements with
yesterday's engagements
So quickly to yes's and right back to maybe's
Call me crazy…
but I am for you—
And in three months it's definitely a maybe
Rating from 1-6 in days contemplating
I think Kendrick said it best…

A "fatal attraction is common and what we have common is pain…"
Let's face it
Leaving each other in more pain when we are angry
Trying to determine if it's worth it or are wasting…time
Who knows??
All I care about is snuggling up under you when the bedroom door closes
Whether we last forever or just enough to cherish right now
No matter what I'll never let you down
3-19-13

Our Love

You're becoming like my best friend,
The one I ride for, I'd die for, go in and out for,
Like it's a sin,
Falling out just to fall back in,
Yeah we winnin'....
Tag-teaming tables just to make sure we insure each other's hand,
-sighs-... can you tell I'm in love?
You're like my night stand...
Holding me down when no one else can,
Stacking building blocks on OUR master plan,
Me to you, and you to me equals #1 fan,
Living the story written beforehand,
Battling missions; my battle buddy disguised as my mistress,
Turned lover through a few kisses,
And hopefully one day addressed as the (Mrs.)
That'll allow me to cast back and reminisce
On every tear, bit of fear, and things we hold dear were clearly worth it,
Understanding there was never a need for soul searching,

As a TEAM we made our own love into PERFECT!

Tattered Heart

Speak to my heart
Cause lately it's been going deaf
The proposed love that once set is dead!
And my heart is no longer hears soft whispers
In fact it has a block on love long distance
You know the love that fades far off in the background along with hugs and kisses
The lead on promises that turn to broken wishes
And then it's left here
Pulsating through tears
Heart beats a minute seem to speed up by fear
Searching for answers but none seem so clear

The Enemy

Why do I find myself wondering?
Writing your name tons of times all over my paper down in front of me
Going back over each line just to make sure the rhyme has become of me
[Chuckles] … I find it funny
Cause as I tell myself "there's no way you can move forward"
My feet find the path and guide my heart on towards you
Warmth of the feeling makes it sound so corny, but it's true
I don't just casually think of an us…
I've mapped a 5 year plus plan and scheduled you for the remainder of our knowing
You see my idea of you
"forever" hasn't even began
Just seems to be another story
I'm here sorting out my weaknesses so we can approach this plan,
soaring across the sky , like it's our morning
Don't want nothing or no one to take this feeling away

Begging just to hear you say, you're here to stay
The fear of losing you would give me a room to result to mourning
I'd be doomed if you shot this glory
See, I want to define for you exactly what it feels
when your heart starts racing because the words cut tears
I don't want to have to say, when actions speak louder than words anyway
You're an addition to one of my good thangs
They say all good things come to an end eventually
I believe that's only when it goes unappreciated
So, I'm here to demonstrate differently,
I want to give you a reason to believe that it's real
Just believe me
I want to gain back your trust, let you know I'm not the enemy.

Dedicated to: E. N. Fields

The "N" Crowd

It was instant,
Every line that shaped you defined
DIFFERENT!
Every word you spoke,
The not-so-funny jokes,
Told me <u>THIS</u> wouldn't go any further than friendship.
I needed an outlet,
And for once this wasn't just a rebound project.
You easily strided along a broken object with means of making it whole,
NO ONE had ever done that!
I mean sure they spoke on the deed
And everything in between,
You know the "you deserve better"
But not willing to show you, EVER.
For the most part, sex was the only scheme,
But with you it was quite a mystery.
You stood out like the ink blots on the dotted paper…
writing out our history.
There was no meshing with the other shades of gray.

The not-so much-like the others stood out blatantly.
Your blank stares saw through my emptiness,
Your first kiss to my lips sent in a rush of adrenaline
You didn't blend in the crowd
You highlighted my smile
For a moment, you managed to alter my mindset that classified you differently…

Dedicated to: J. Dunn

The Only One

My loyalty runs like no other...
Not on 2 feet
But
riverside deep
Like ripples in the ocean
For you
I'm tunnel visioned
I see nothing in my path
I have no time for harmless
recognitions
Critiquing surrounding bodies
That are irrelevant to my mission
My soul breathes, consumes, and digest only
you
On a day filled with gray clouds
Angry words and pounding fists
When temptation draws you South of your
heart's beating rhythm
When pride won't let you apologize
For stepping on me for the 100th time
I still remain true to only you
No time for entertaining conversations
Or enjoying juvenile cravings
That only shade me from pain that I suffer
from on a temporary basis

Real love doesn't settle for petty
But somehow
I still remain in this shuttle
Tussling on some sleepless nights
Alone ..
Waiting…
Ready….
for when you're ready…
It'll be too late.

Love Can Be

New love
can be bold, intense, and exciting.
Filled with joy,
new butterflies,
hours on hours of conversations,
building friendships,
and solid foundations
beyond what one may envision.
Love can also be toxic, septic, and be filled
with pain.
Festering with deceit,
uncertainties, and insecurities
that two lovers may use
to excuse their actions
all while trying
to shade them with images of love.
It's unexplainable,
And far from a fairy tale
It's challenging ….
I'm in L.O.V.E
6-11-13

Our Bond

This is what she does to me
When my mind is racing
It's because she covers me
I flow past the nonsense and she runs with me
Like fork and knife run together because it's cutlery
She rides with me
And we fight
And we grind
With the same mission in mind
It's because of
Her…She...Me…Us…
That we do what we must
Not a broken handle
Or even the perfect mantle could break a bond that we hold so strong
Trust….
I know this "no matter what"
This Capricorn-sag affair can't be tamed
When our names graze the easel
As we retrace our pain
We paint a beautiful picture with our memories in vain
And in the rain we rinse off the excess

Making room for the next day's faults and blessings
Recalling the lessons before we lay to rest
Thanking GOD for being by our side
And praying to rise
Just in time for the next day…
So that we can conquer the world together
5-8-13

What Happened?

I find myself wondering often
We didn't meet by coincidence?
…there is in fact a purpose
I hate that the last 6 weeks have been a test though
Lord knows ..
my heart but I promise bashing in a skull was surely a thought
Sometimes I find myself wondering what really happened.
3-18-13

Why I Love You

When you ask me why I love you
I swear to GOD love has no reason
The way you make me smile, the way you treat me
The way you keep my heart beating
The cold feeling that runs through my body when you tell me how you feel
It's just the little things baby that drives me crazy, you keep it real.
The way I'm missing you, the pointless arguments, the salty tears I've cried after fights
The break-ups to make-ups, the "I love you's" that fall throughout the night
Your jealousy, your selfishness, the path you wish for me,
I strive to keep us bonded together 'cause your love is all I breathe.
So, when you ask me why I love you I put my heart in for you to see.

Unpredictable

I wish you knew me better than you already think you do
The eyes that aren't mine when you look into the two
The lips design to lie syncing all you wanna hear
The cold transited to heat that blows upon your ear
The brushed upon blush, tint to the hair
Eyes lined with mascara just to cover up the tears
Lips lined perfect so that when I smile no fear is detected
The only way I know that my heart is protected
The only way known to feel accepted
Like a good fix, washing up pain with pain
Now I'm crying for change and affection
So take away the liner, the gloss, the style, the outer me
Strip away the lies, the fear and start accepting reality
Accept my truth for real and feel my relief
Know this insider you knew nothing about before; for me

You've Lost

She is battered…
because of you.
From the inside out
Her heart is bruised black and blue
It shows
Even through her glistening smile
And choice of clothes
The world still knows
She's in love
She loves everything
About you
The way you look at her when you desire her
And even when you don't
Even the way you scold at her minute mistakes
Because she knows
Eventually you will start to love her again
Falling out of love just to fall back in
Going through the motions just to get through them
Reducing her to inferior
And putting other bitches in the front seat
While she struggles in the rear
Shoving her down the stairs

Pulling at her hair
Hitting below the belt to make her feel that you don't care
Being an asshole
Remaining selfish
Thinking the world revolves around your bullshit
Bringing her to tears,
reinforcing her fears
Crashing her confidence
Because an ego stroke is what you would rather be down with
Enjoying the 20, instead of the 80
Because right now it's the best fit
Yea she loves all of that shit
But trust in due time
The heart that is so filled with love
Will explode
There will be no shape to hold
This constant overflow
She will continue to do her part
Until her heartbeat closes doors
A loyal bitch is her only code
So keep doing everything just the way she likes it
No affection,

no "I love you's"
Keep fucking with those temporary items
bitches who couldn't light up your corner
even if you turned on the flash and guided them
Just keep on fighting with her
She likes it best
Knowing in the back of your dysfunctional mind
To you it's just a test
That when you get tired
You'll climb right behind her
expecting her to once again
Put the shit behind the hurt
sweep it under the rug
Disregard the "bad love"
Because it was just another episode
chuckles
It's funny ...
As your urge to be single back folds
Blackjack tables can't even account for your toll
So sad that you just hang on to such hope
Hanging on thin rope
Because you just know
She's not going anywhere

But how could you be so sure?
With no recollection that you pay the cost
you have no idea
That you've already lost.

Where I'm Going:
(further, deeper, darker)

Almost

Stop being selfish
invading my feelings for your well being
while you're scheming
shedding light on other fish
while I still hold temporary hopes of us
being...
I almost slipped up today
just because I heard you say
you wanted to see me
but thank God for all the hurt you caused
because it strengthen me to dodge your
faulty image in the meeting
I love you , that's no secret
I crave your lips and touch by day
but I pray for strength to push me over to
keep me from running back your way
I pray for growth in your direction so that
you can unlearn your tainted views
and treat the next flex like the best yet
because no one should ever have to choose
as long as I'm to willing wait for your
change you will never level up
and as I much as I give
and as much as I love
it just will never be enough

I need you to see what life without me does
for your soul and mental frame
because the time we invested into each other
can never be regained
B.Maree 8-2-16

Blindsided- NPM #1

I'm trying to balance it
The pain that silently seeps through the cracks of me
While appearing to be happy
Shit…
I'm just acting
Using props to hold me up
While inside I'm steadily crashing
Trying to pick up my fallen self
From trippin' down your faulty pathway
Pushing quickly pass the lies
Filled with rage and part confused
Questioning my worth and self-respect
And all the things I have to lose
Replaying scenes in my mind that I thought would last forever
Trusting in you to lead me to our mutual goals
Climbing through the past whatever's
Building mustard seed capabilities that would carry us throughout our different means
Ending up with disappointments that counter set our future dreams

Beating myself up for allowing you to build me up just to tear me down
Asking myself how could I be so blind to miss the sign you through around?

Empty (Themed Writing)
I wanted to believe that it existed
So… I handed you the needle and asked you to stitch it
And after everything that I had been through
I thought that you would be able to fix it
So many broken pieces needed mending…
instead of curving the needle around the broken ends
You dug the sharp point deeper and created more open wounds than sealing them
Emptied out all of its contents and after that still kept digging
Tearing at the seams as if something was missing
The only things that filled it were
Memories of us every time you were forgiven
-chuckles-
Silly rabbit still haven't learned yet...
Time moves forward and waits for no one so why waste your time on a setback
Lessons are brought to you but never truly processed...
Your breaking point was losing her

And in the midst your pain caused you to hurt me
Laying on my back so that you could rise above it
Yet I'm still sinking

Falling in Love

Struggling to hold it together
Stay in place when emotions turn high
Be a friend before anything
Recalling the reasons I chose to get onto this ride
I'm so over the temperament coverage
Back and forth between interim lovers
Building memories up
just to test on the luck
Though we'll never rise above what hovers
Patterns are in the air...
warnings are hardly rare
Feelings immiscible
Cause when I'm missing you, missing me, missing you
You act like you don't even care
Didn't expect to fall ocean deep
Now I'm swimming pass coral reefs
With each stroke of the motion
Up and down roller coasters
For the words you'll never hear me speak.

Fight's Not Over

I find that she wants me to give her up
Pointing out flaws that she hasn't accepted
As she crutches on the excuses of her past pain reflecting
It's because she hasn't experienced real love
Every attempt has disabled her
And nothing but doubts have consumed her conscience
Tricking her into believing she isn't worthy
Comparing her lack of equivalence to be less than deserving
She doesn't recognize that my staying is for her heart
Not a financial gain
Or come up from her story
I'm here because I believe
I stay because I understand
I vowed a forever even without the wedding band
I love without reason even after outlining why I'm here
My aim is to show her that I'm here to heal
And that there's nothing here to fear
Until there's nothing left to battle
And my heartbeat fails to sync

The fight is far from over
Because I'm still standing in the ring.

Flat Line

I wanna believe that everything happens for
a reason
every move made was dead spot
for a more appropriate season
that you refused to bare humility
and I hunted just to feel the pain
and every phone call that rang through
skipped heartbeats
as I rushed to pick up
just to hear you say
"why can't we just be friends"......

Forbidden Crush

This invisible bite of your apple has me under
The juices I'll never taste has spellbound me into oblivion
Your skin that I can't touch
Your lips that I can't kiss
Your hug I'll never feel
Your eyes I'll never stare in
The words that I'll never hear because
Admitting to you the feeling that I crave is forbidden

Expired

We had an expiration date
Just like everything else
It went bad.
Nearing the shelf life
Only drew us closer to the edge of jumping
As we pushed closer to the ledge
While new emotions filed behind ....

Here

how did we get here
with subtle conversations
and skin to skin abrasions
how did we exchange cold nightmares
for warm intense concentrations
conversations that led to
lips-locked
hands cocked
for sweet honey pepper tracings over
dress-less skin
back seat grubbing
heavy panting and
dancing through the clouds as we
climaxed to the open crowd
seeing just us
because it was just about us
intentions of friend things
only on the weekends
karaokin' our way through each other's
deep seas
looking pass the past and current secrets
only to rock back and forth into our own
ship
friend-ship
court-ship

co-habit--ship
now we are into the deepest
of this shit
loving each other through the deepest grips
and
stomaching the days
when we make each other both sick
and caring for each other
as if we are just what the doctor ordered
throwing back scripts
tracing back our steps
to the moment we first met
where threads about snapbacks
turned into commentary slips
leading to inboxes
and face timing
and short-handed responses
all from a picture that
said
"girl come and find me "
on some creep dip
late night garage sips
car vibin ,
night owl
planning to be mine
in due time

no matter the consequence
that's how we got here

Let Go

I tell myself everyday
It's okay that your feelings have changed
I'm just gonna have to force myself to
understand that you don't feel the same
I lie to myself every night when I climb into
my bed
That laying in the dark alone is better
Than laying next to you instead
I've convinced myself that maybe, just
maybe someone else is right for you
She will come into your life and her spirit
will move you to change your views
She will open your heart to see that
commitment isn't such a scare
And you'll make the conscious effort
To cherish her and always be there
I tell myself that who's meant for me
Will show up in due time
I'll be showered with queen like inferences
and they'll appreciate the "ride or die"
I tell myself to look deeper and understand
Nothing is always meant to last
And that the time was far from wasted
It helped prepare for what's to pass

I can't tell you that what's needed isn't disguised in mistress prints
Or that your journey ends with me because I've watered all your lengths
I'll just keep telling myself
What makes you happy keeps me happy in between
I can't open your eyes to point out everything you haven't seen
Because if seeing it on your own means exposing the blind to visible sights
Who gives a fuck about what I think
When you're not willing to write your wrongs into rights
I can't open up your eyes
And even though I know this
I'm so sick of allowing myself to hear you out
Repeating the same tired lines
With that same selfish vibe
Knowing this shit here has got to stop
I can't convince you that your love runs symmetrical to my heart's rhythmic beat
I can't change you or tame you into the woman that I want you to be

For every heartbreak, I just remind myself that whatever its worth I'm willing to set you free
And I tell myself this because no matter how hard I try be
We will never be as happy if you can't find what you're looking for in me
But no matter how many times I tell myself the lies I've told before
I've come to the realization
I'm not ready to let go

Mask Off

You don't get it
My pain isn't symmetrical to how it's written
Aside from my complaining
and bitchin
My scars hold memories that are far deeper than rivers
You think I'm tripping
Because happy memories bless your timeline with smiles and giggles
But pictures only cover up for what's really missing inside
Masking tragedy has always been a perfect disguise

Master's Journey

Anxiety pushed us over
The need for speed
And correcting mistakes
And being the best
Kept me sober
Countless papers
Late night struggles
Last minute studies
Adamant takeovers
Strong team players
My A1 gamers
Kept me in line
Like a battle soldier
My lifelines vowed to never let me fall flat
On the journey to the top
Although this walk is almost over
There are no plans for us to stop
Motivation from each other
Wouldn't have it any other way
As we line up , robed down, slayed
Prepared to march on to the day
Where our names await embedded plaques
And our pride is leveled high
No matter where our directions take us
I'll always be there by your side.

Dedicated to my awesome classmates that have grown to become family; my sisters: Cobi, Kelly, Jenn, Roxie #4, Rayven with a "Y" and last but not least my big brother Mark!!

Privileged (Theme Writing)

Have you ever heard of black privilege?
Of course not...
What black person of power you know that hasn't been profiled?
Let's talk about the job applications that keep US from jobs
Or the truth, our color of skin keeps them terrified
They undermine our strength
Hell once upon a time we were considered just three-fifths
Not even looked at as a whole person
Kept underway
serving their nights
Slave by day
Ask a person of European descent if white privilege exist
And watch what they say
They've never had to experience the disadvantage
Of driving while black
While we are constantly asking
What did we do wrong
Their response
"be born"

See we don't belong on the very soil that doesn't belong to them
Power and prestige has kept them above all men
Crazy part, they don't even know it
So ask me what does privileged mean?
That right there just goes to show you…

Second Guess

the idea of having forever seems so far away
when everything you ever wanted
had once been in your palm
but crumbled like ash at the ending of the story
no happily ever after planned as you had dreamt
looking for replacements to fill places of people long gone
promises made. broken;
because fulfilling them would have been far more damaging than committing to the lies
you swapped interchangeably for comfort
love and orgasms that only brought rise in the heat
how convenient of you to think bearing a seed would suffice as permanency
that 10 months of growth inside your inner lining would mean someone could finally love you back
how selfish of you to think you are ready for that?
not once did you pause to think could this fetus come into your fuck'd up world and survive this wrath

your mental anguish swelling bigger than
the pump of the vessels in your chest
dead bolts equivalent to the beat below your
breast
You might want to second guess that

She Is

The look in her eye says it all
She has had ENOUGH.
She is tired
Of crying
Of pretending to be tough
Of being brushed aside due to
The lack of your love
Of just going with the flow
Of pretending she doesn't know
That you are playing with her heart,
so...
If hurt people, hurt people
Then just let her go.

Stimulation (Themed Writing)
Lay down and relax
Close your eyes and get comfortable while I caress you on your back
Tracing my fingers through your spine
Massaging pressure points through your line
And slowly inching on down
To spread the two
Dividing both hemispheres to see what it does to you
Peering through the veins to determine which one you frequently use
Slowly I move my fingers in between
Finding my way through your most dominant dreams
Figuring out how to make you mentally scream
Tracing your track looking to examine how and why you think like you think
Act like you act
Digging deeper for the G spot that sits in your brain
Penetrating the sensitive areas that air out your pain
Rising you above all that you overcame

Watching you explode in my thoughts at the thought of this aim
Slowly
Carefully...
Refilling your thought process
With new access to securities you were unaware of
So....
Relax
sit up and open your eyes
Tell me all about your cries
When the journey takes a left
Just know I'll be over here on the right

Success

Success is more than earning your place
Success is more than a smile on your face
Success is more than just proving you're good
Success is your guider if you're not quite understood
Success is more than beat in our lives
Success is more than just a beam out of the sky
Success is more than just reaching the top
Success is the reason you've got what you've got.

Teach Me

I want you to teach me how to be just like you
How to lie, how to make promises, but never fall through
How to spit venom vials and tear your heart right down to shreds
And spend hours ignoring you because I know it fucks with your head
I want you to teach me how to walk in your shoes
Creep through the house at the midnight hours
After I've rummaged through your food
I want you to teach me how to go out and leave you swarming in your thoughts
Teach me how to lay with another woman, while thinking of you, and still not get up
Teach me how to spit the game that gets my ego stroked
How to leave my good thang at home.
And settle for what the streets call.
I'm begging you to teach me how to climb into your sheets at night
And repeat the same ol' lines
That "I love you" and "I need you"

After I've broken you down for the 1000th time
Teach me how to trigger all of your weakened points
So that I know even after I've fucked up I can still call this home
Teach me how to be so disrespectful that I blatantly talk to other women when you're there
How to disregard your feelings even though I know that it's not fair
Teach me how to make believe that you don't even exist
How to look at the last 2 years as if it were "just some other shit"
Teach me how to stop loving you
How to sit back, chill & do me
How to look right through your shattered pieces and walk right pass them while you bleed
Teach me how to use you to my everyday advantage
That when I leave you and come back I'll know that I still have it
Teach me so that when you realize your heart no longer beats

You'll recognize the hurt you feel is ALL
you put in me.

The Comeback
How real was this??
Even through the worst shit
I expected you to let me cry, rant, hurt, and vent
but leaving my side
instead of being my ride or die
wasn't what I expected ...
even you said it takes time
plenty of it....
or has, the time really come to rid of "us"...
time waits for no one
and everyone has pain
been racking my brain with the fear of the unknown and in some form resenting you
but more disappointed in myself for trusting you with my temple...
loving you has never faded
although never anticipated I'm glad that we made it..
to experience some form of life although a struggle
the strife has never been so worth it...
hearing you utter "it's not worth it" was maybe what I needed

to release me of the heartache that I often felt beating
maybe I've just been lying to myself
trying to make decisions in between lies and discomfort...
making excuses for your hurt and reckless bullshit
in need of that companionship...
buying it all because I felt "even in the bad you were all that I had"
but now I'm feeling alone
numb to the cycles of the last 7 weeks
so weak that I can't even stand to my feet--
and walk.
I can't even raise my finger to point out what stands out anymore
no energy to close doors
I'm just numb to this crazy type of love!
So if it's ending let's find a mutual closure...
express the ends and leave the doors wide open
to stand to our feet –
and find the energy to walk out and leave!

Tiger

They say a tiger doesn't change its
stripes
it just grows
My soul is sold
No matter how you add it up
How many times the lies have been divided
into half-truths and promises
that were never held up
I still tried to look past your imperfections
Sticking around awaiting your changes for
the better
Enduring your paw grip because I thought it
was what I was supposed to do
As you sunk your teeth into my heart and
withdrew every emotion that I put into you
Staring in my eyes
Reiterating the lies
Not knowing that
I blindly became the prey
Accepting the tiger's stripes

Unexpected

I opened up my heart
yet again
Trying to clean up the perforated edges
Looking to disguise the battered shell caused by lies
So that once again I could be chosen
Had no hopes of joining another heartless - beat
Lookin' to escape reality
So I told myself this was just a time to gather fun facts
and all that
While I cruised across the playground
Looking forward to the merry go round
The introduction as we twirled in circles spinning small nothings
Into kisses and fondling
Backseat action and cuddlin'
Only to look up and be in love again by morning
So fast that everything now seems blurry
Jumped off the ride feeling dizzy and wobbling
Trying to balance myself while holdin' on to your story

Your pain, your dysfunction, your discomfort
While sweet nothings turn into something
Playground fades into a dungeon
Facing unexpected
dark, cold becoming's
All because I love you....

War Wound
I wanted to believe in you
So I flushed away the memories of the past pain
And stood up again to walk beside you
And out of the blue
Pop...
there the bullet grazed the curve of my heart
No name written in its steel
But it felt real
enough for me to believe
That day it was meant for me
The sting of the of the wound left me stiff
Once again you cocked the gun and set it off just when I wasn't looking.

Weight

I needed an ear to listen
Because I felt so broken deep inside
Betrayed misused and ridiculed
By someone who I thought was here for life
You took my words and spread them across
My eyes for me to see
That the very love I cried about
Was dead weight and pain to me

Why Me?
I've been patient
longing for the love to be reciprocated
Wondering why was I the chosen one
to suffer this season
With so many reasons
You still can't even utter
"Us"
Thinking about me is overrated
Craving for me is beyond you
Fighting for me is not even an option
I am...
Not a priority
No work put in
Just…
used and abused
Wondering if it were never me
Would it have been her
And would single life have been a better choice
Or at least dodging your toxic appeal
Would I have paid less of the cost?

Why You

It's because I love the way your butter cream
skin feels
But not on top of me
I like the feel of how your cheeks seep in
when I rub the back of my hand
to wipe the tears streaming from your
jawline to your chin
That's how I know you're scared of me
eyes pinched tight so that I can't read the
bloodshot lines
while you grit your teeth
pushing me away so you can gather your
thoughts
While I overlap your lap, and rub my hand
through your brittle carpet hair
In an attempt to get you to stare
Still you refuse to connect the glare
Angry with me?
How dare?
Allowing you to walk away with a packed
bag would be me taking the easy way out
so let's shout
back and forth,
about who's right and who's wrong
let's go on and on

until we are breathless
from locking lips
that exchanged hurtful words and profanity
turned to saliva and bite marks
and more grips
for that angry kiss
that tells you to back the fuck down
because it doesn't end like this
not now; not ever!

www.ingramcontent.com/pod-product-compliance
Lightning Source LLC
LaVergne TN
LVHW051606070426
835507LV00021B/2804